CHRISTMAS

COLORING BOOK FOR KIDS

Vol.2

COLOR TEST PAGE

COLOR TEST PAGE

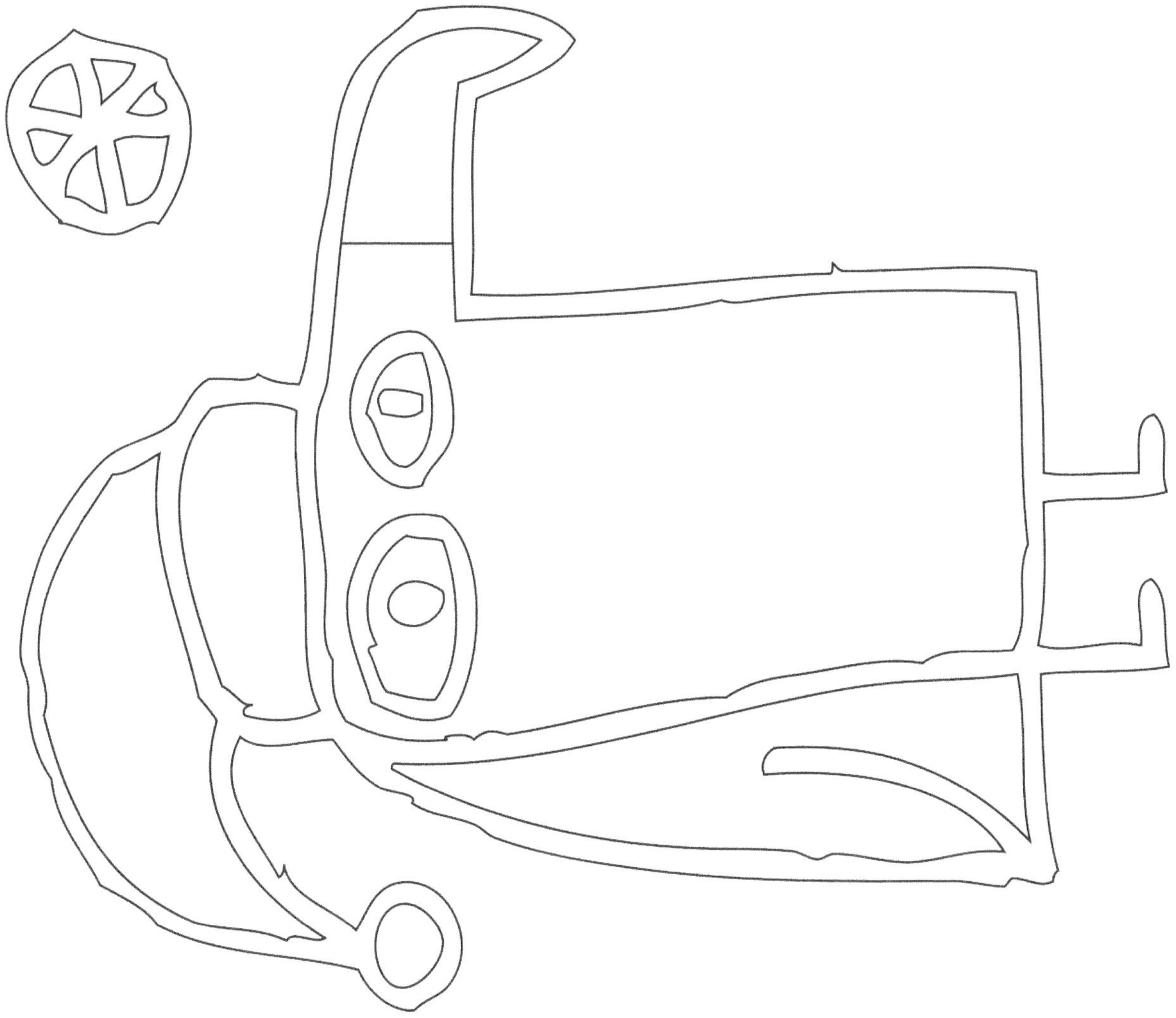

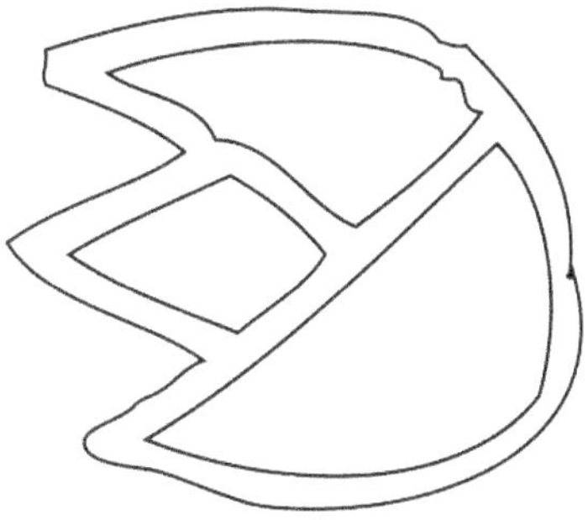

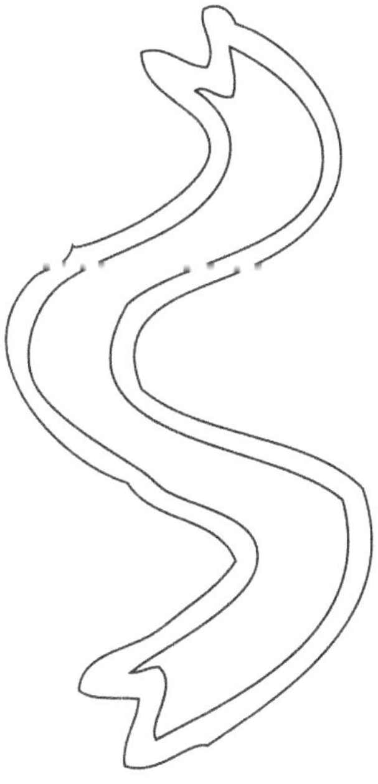

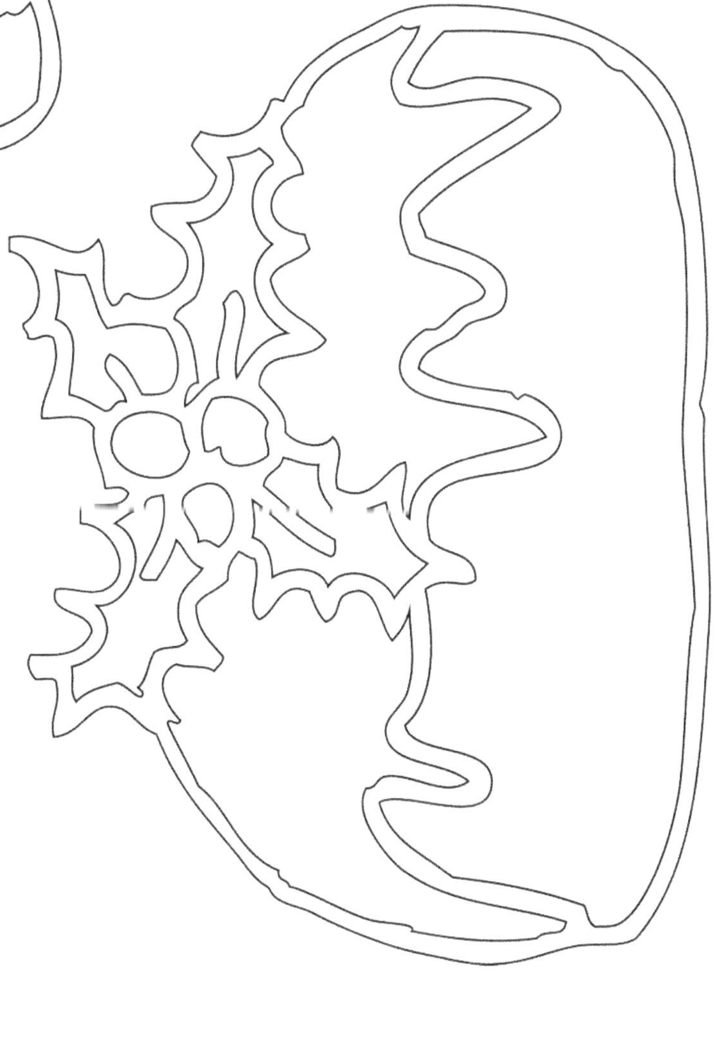

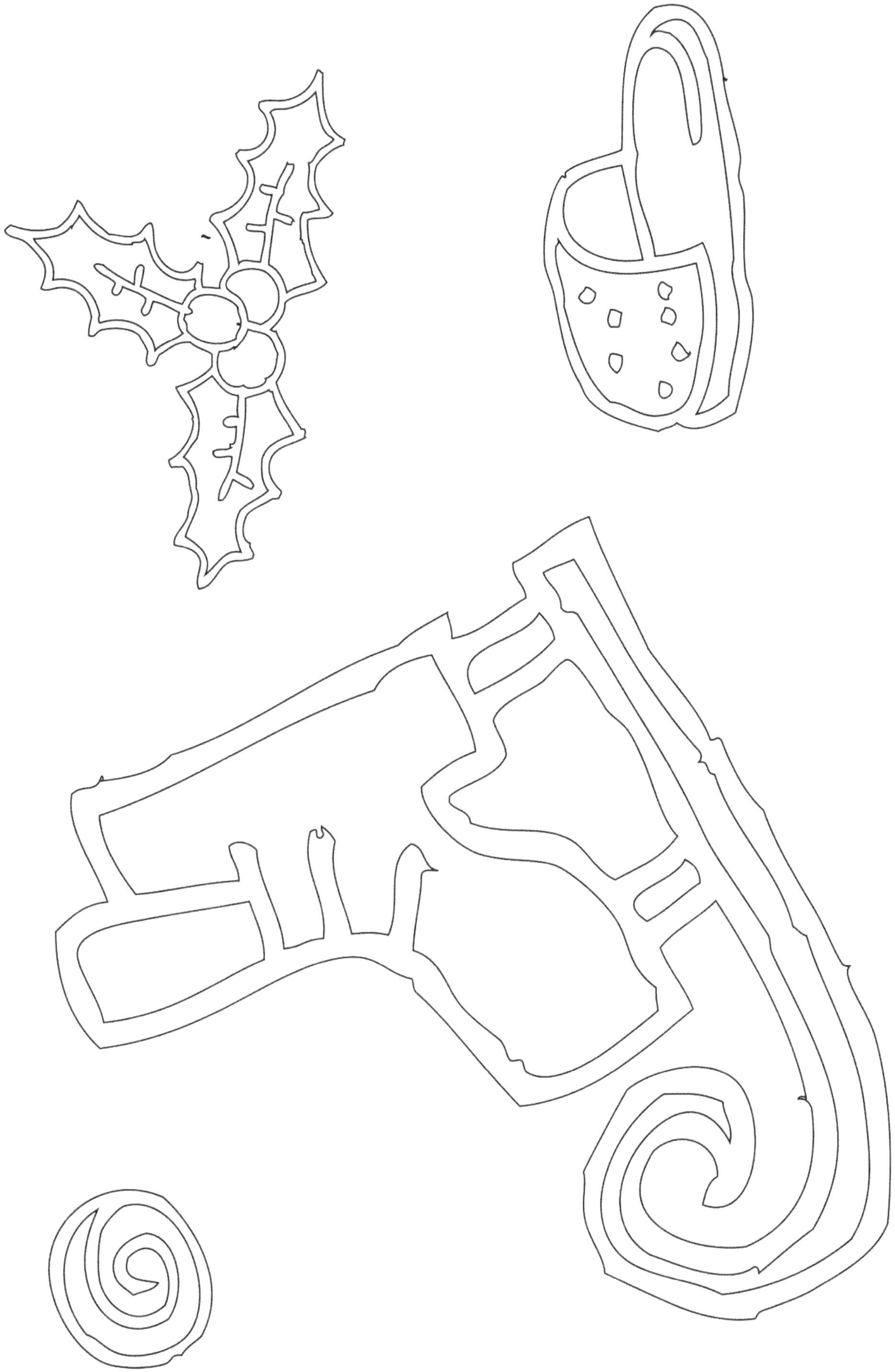

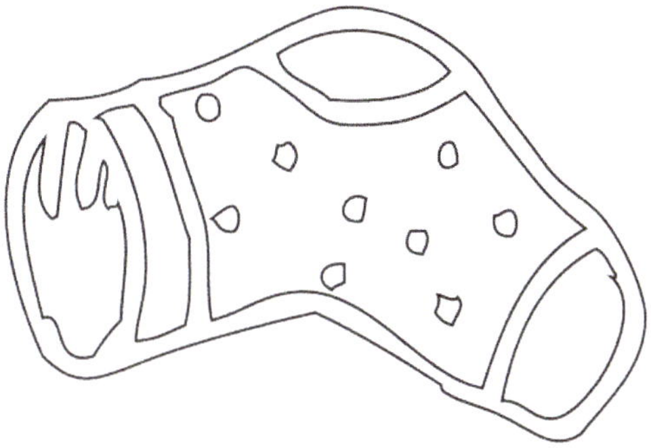

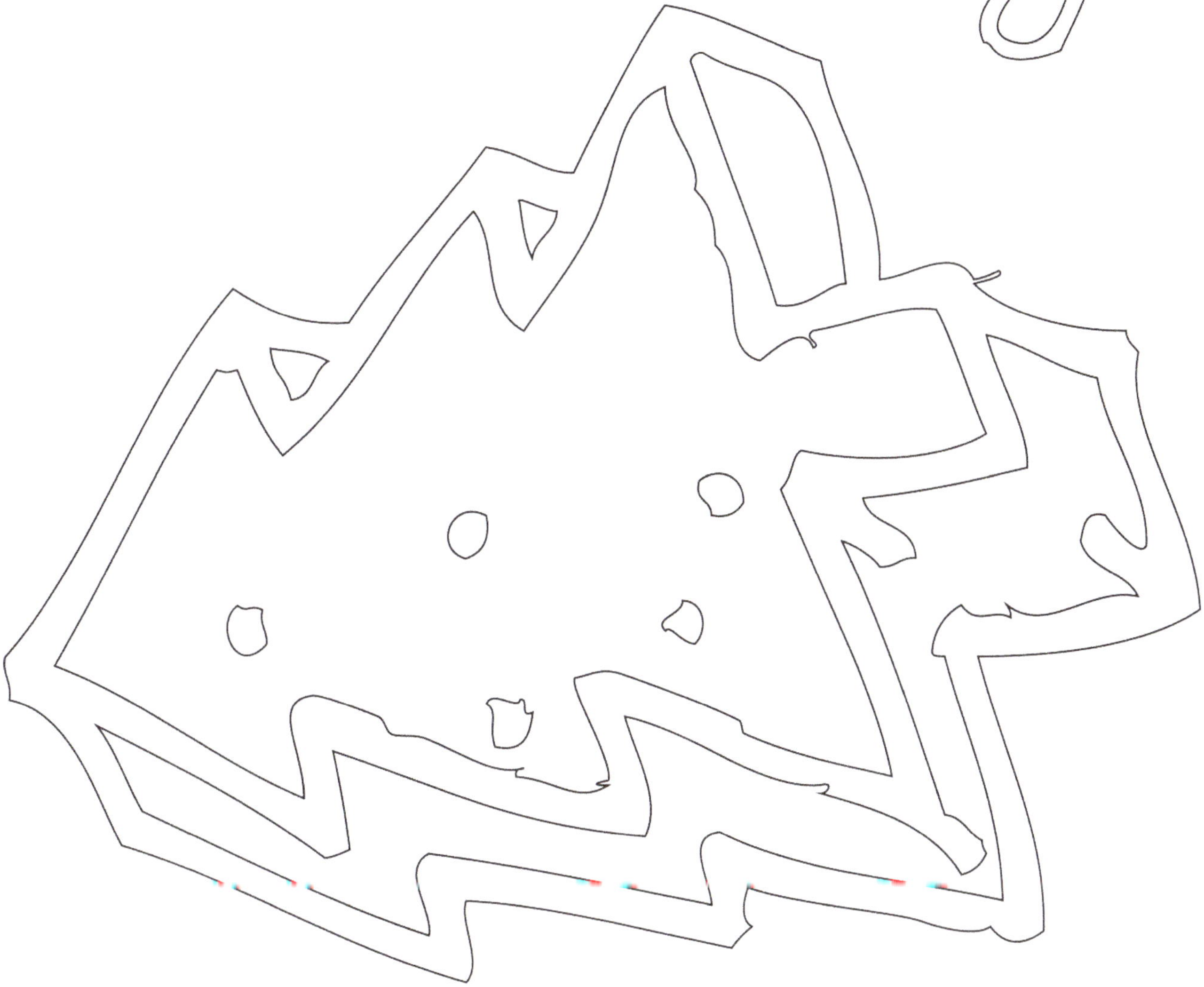
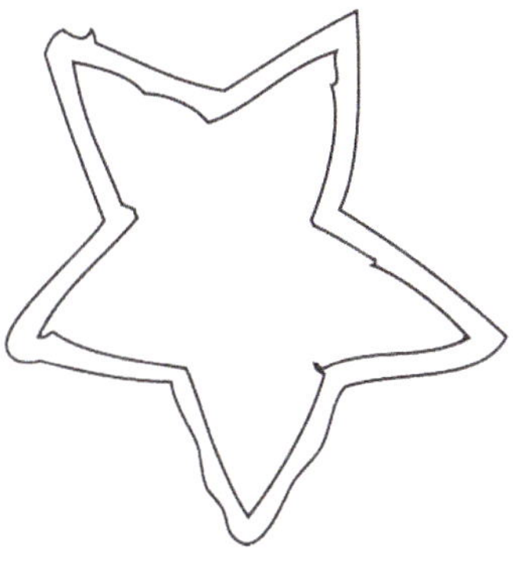

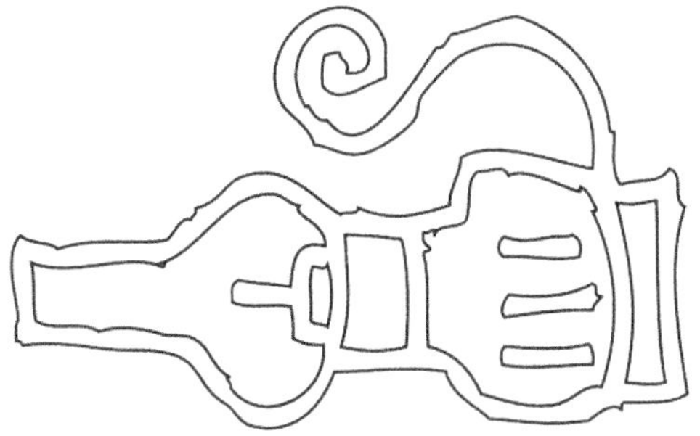

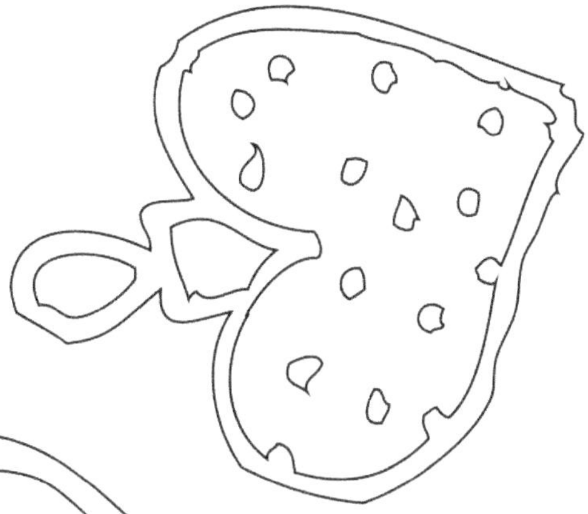

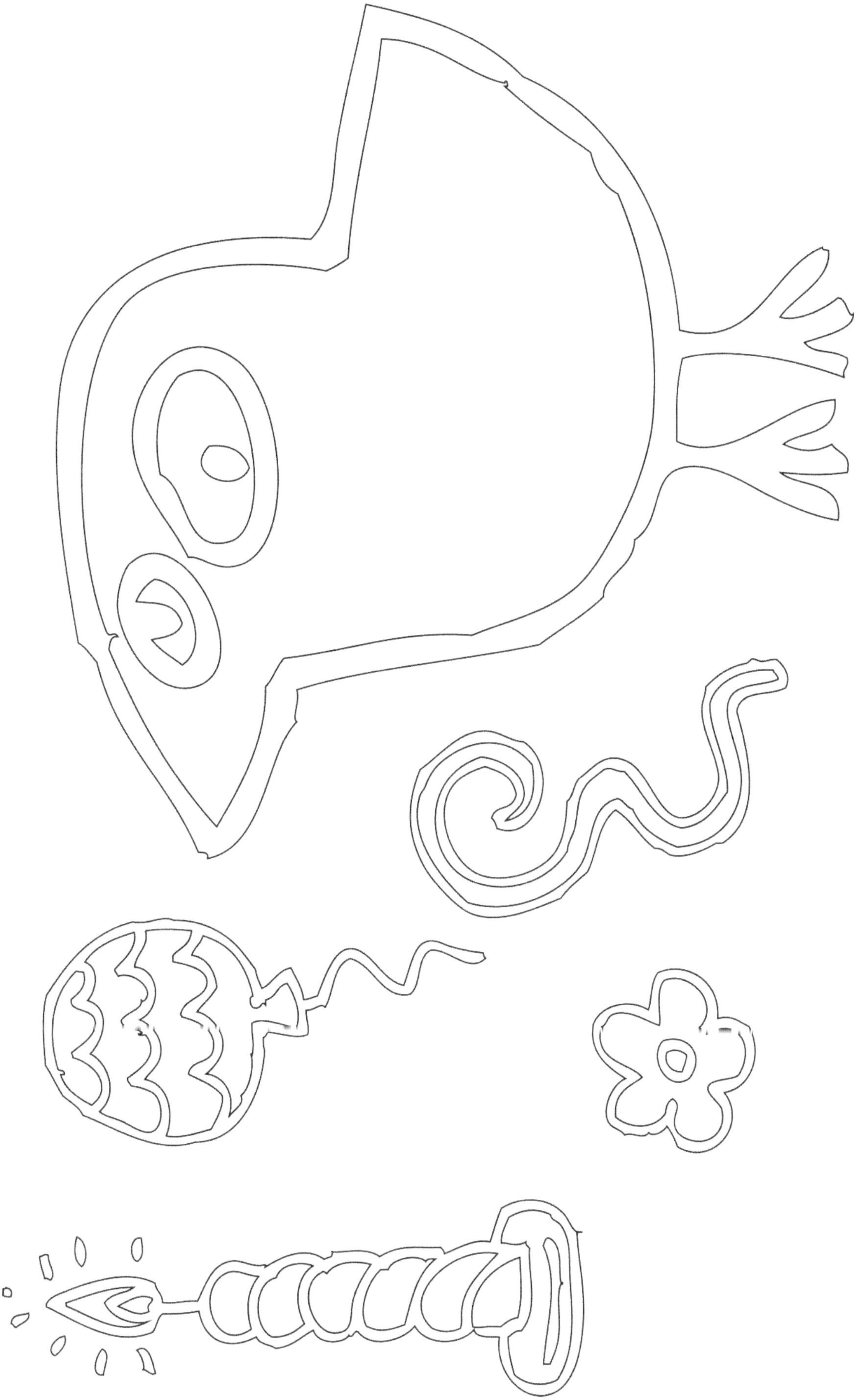

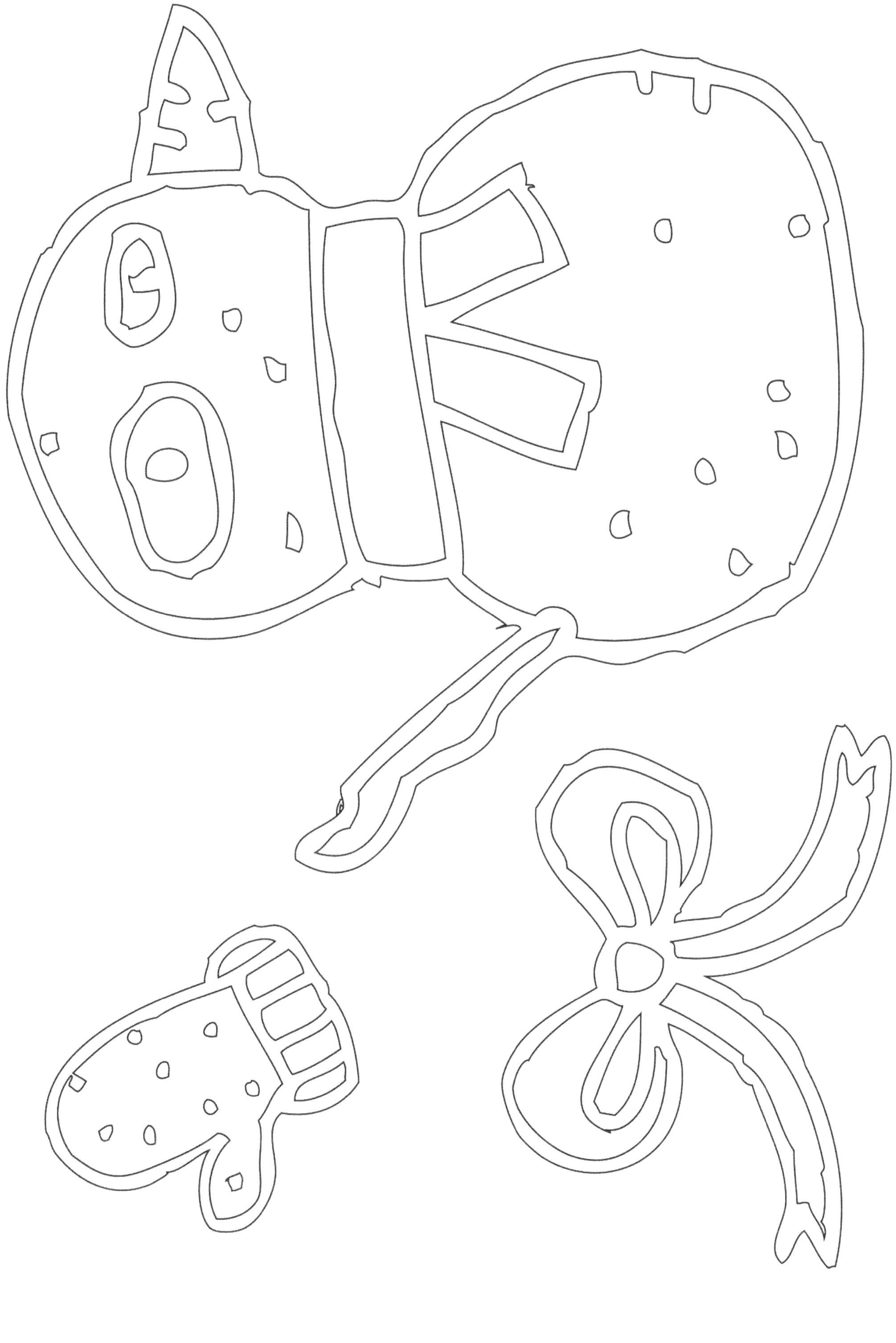

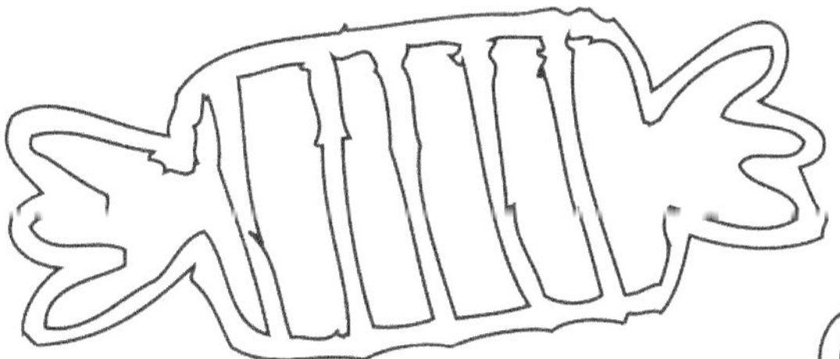

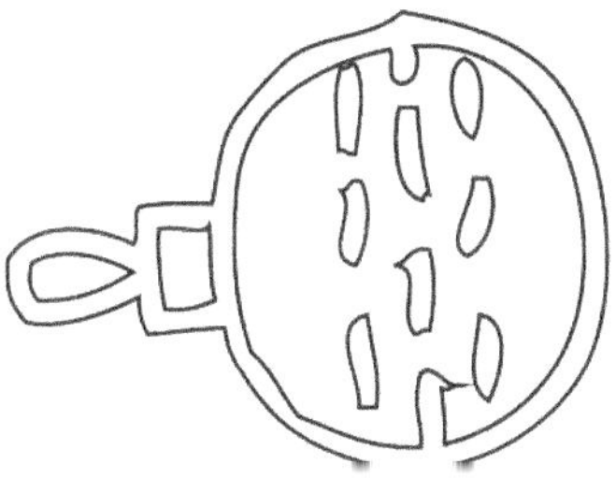

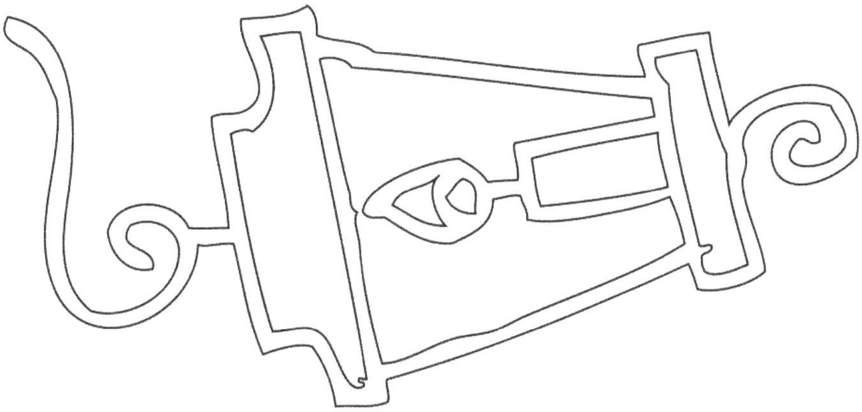

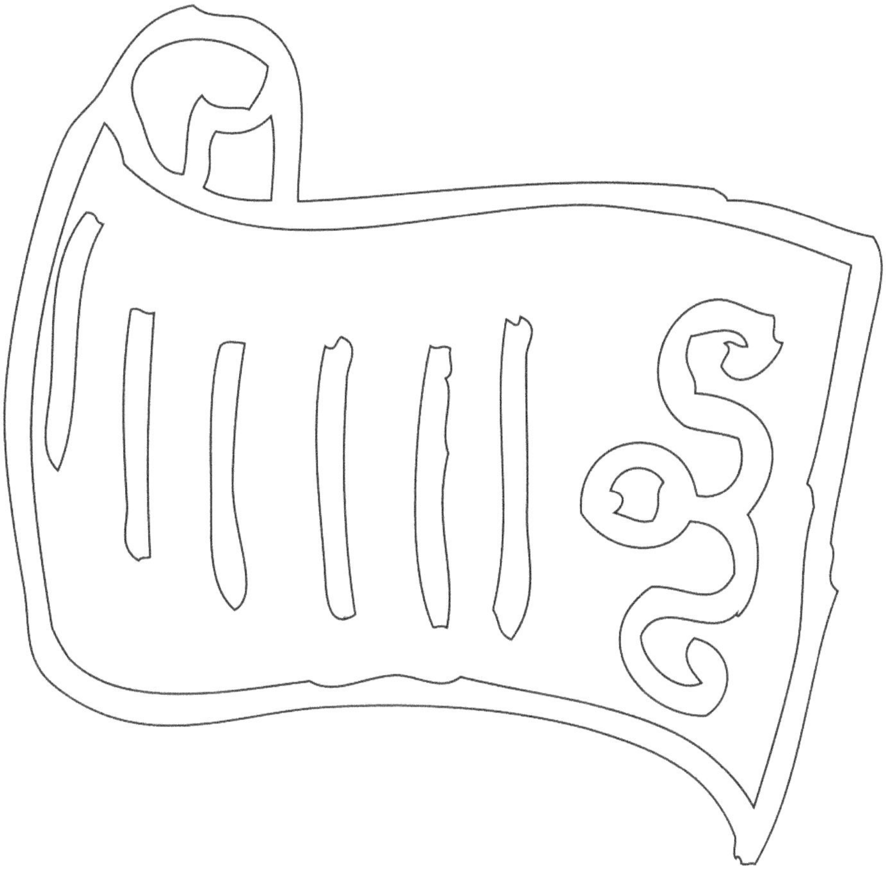

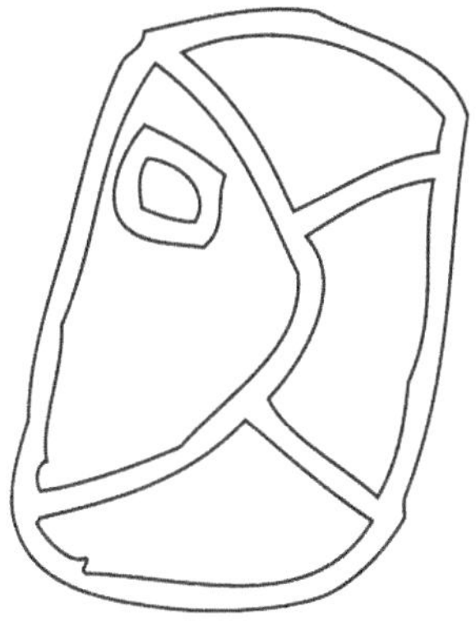

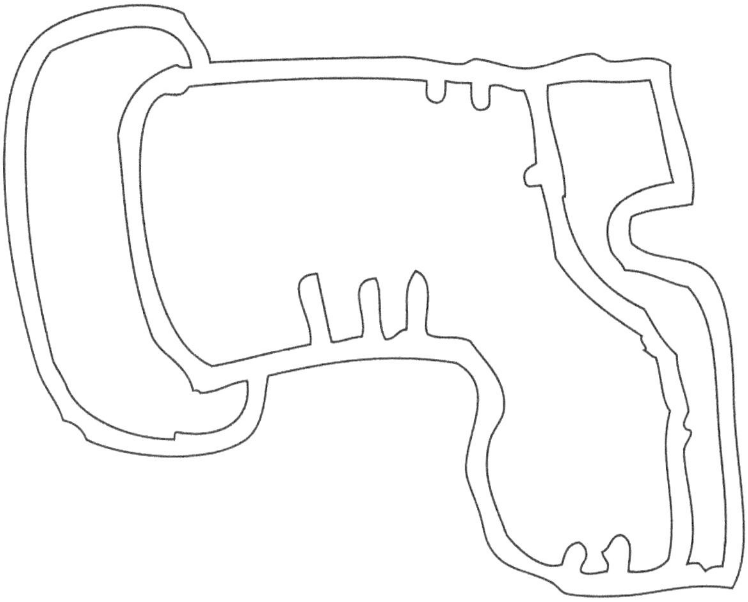
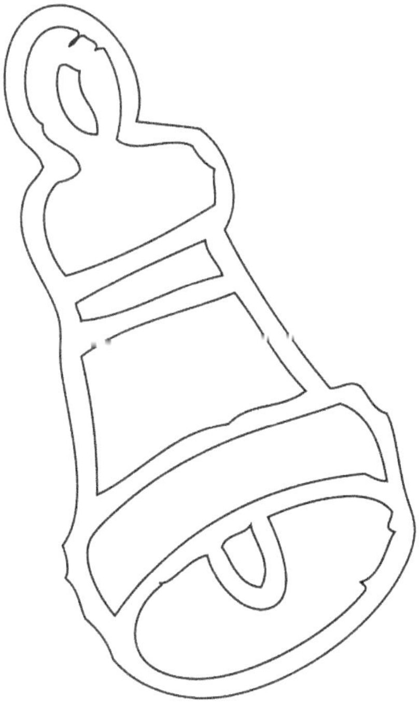

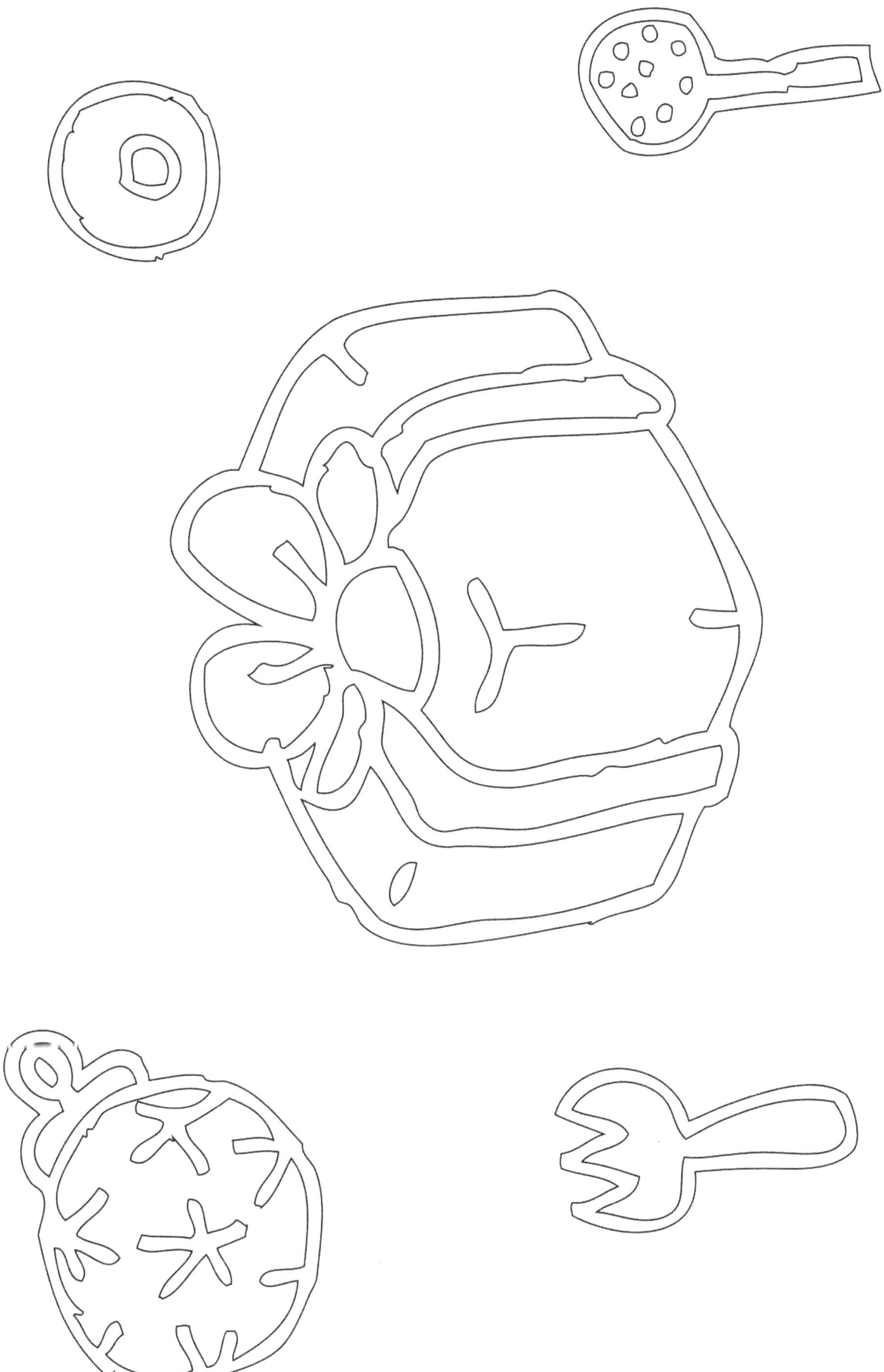

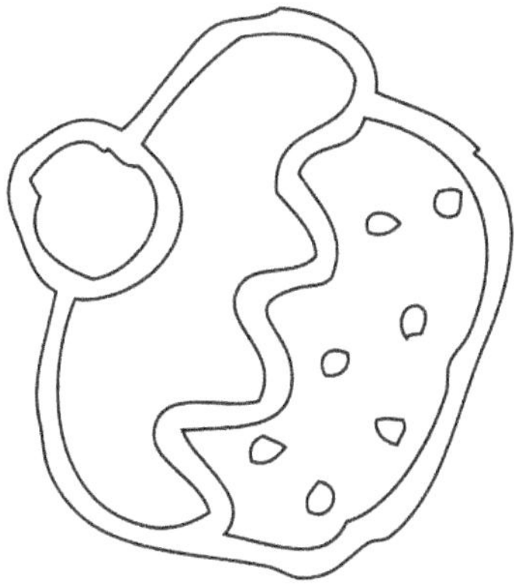
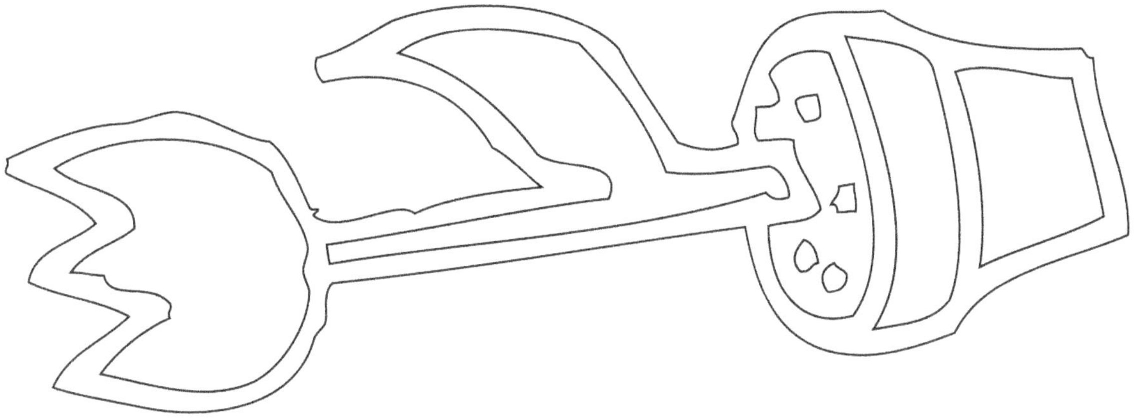
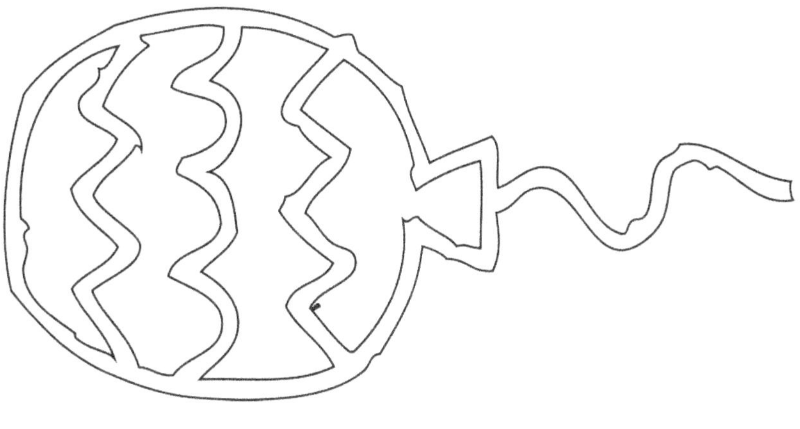

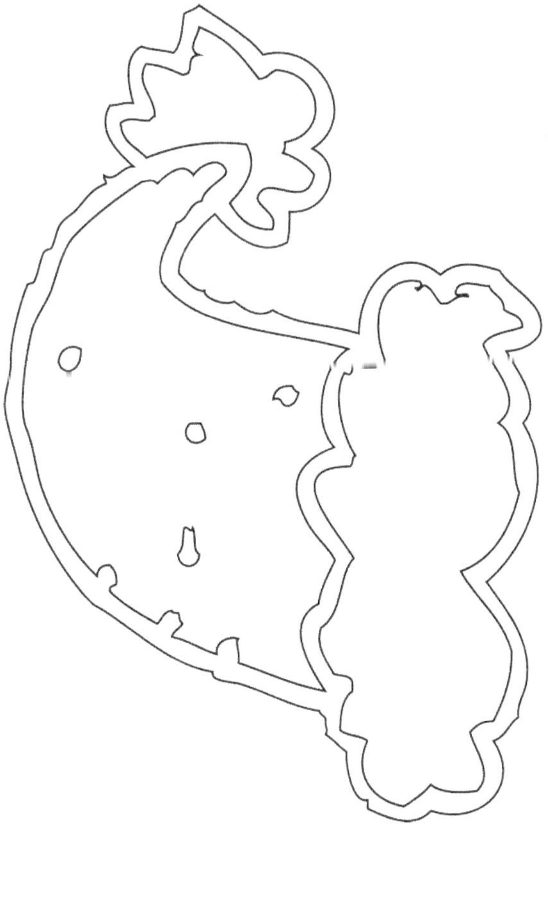

Merry Christmas

Merry Christmas

Merry Christmas

MERRY
CHRISTMAS

MERRY
CHRISTMAS

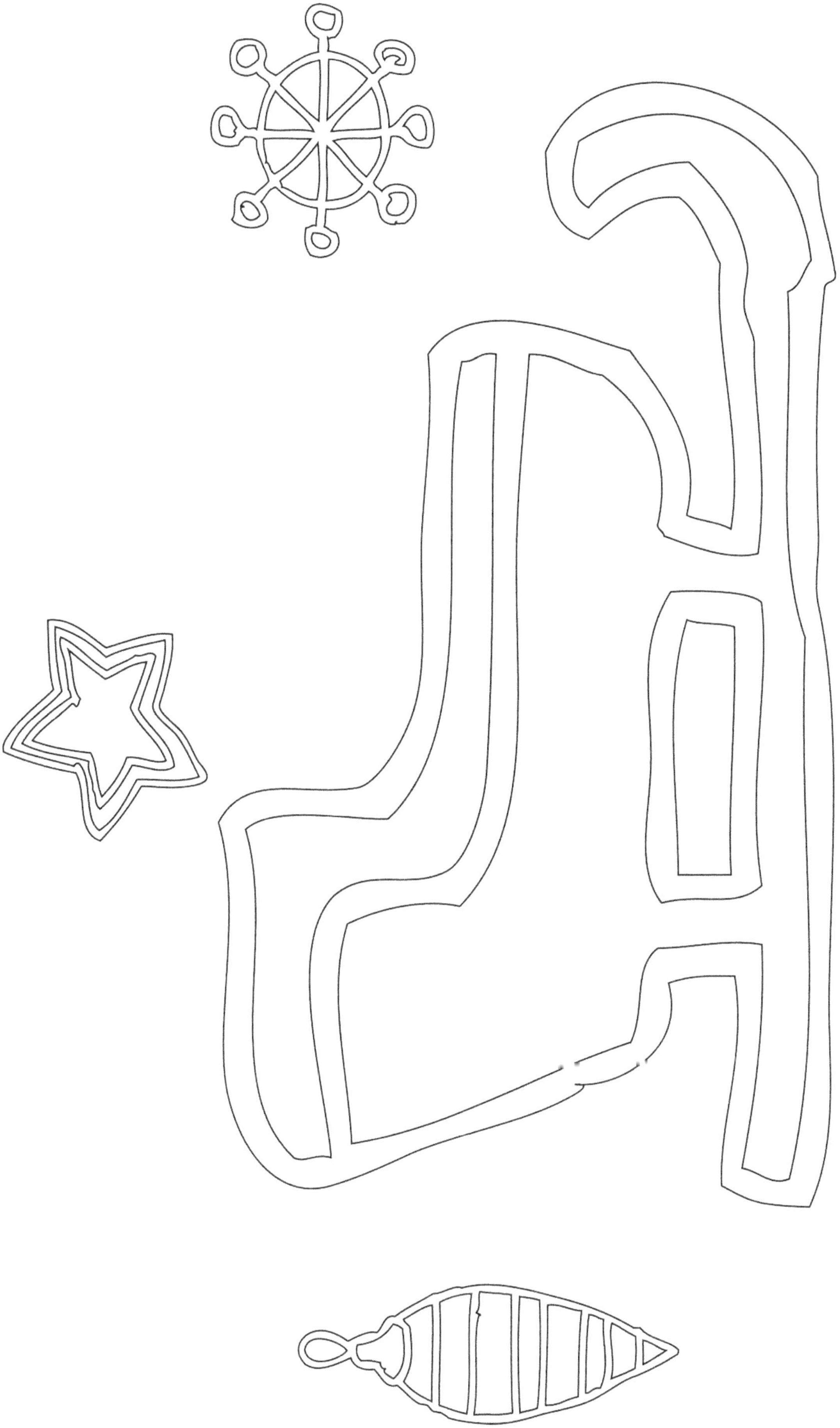

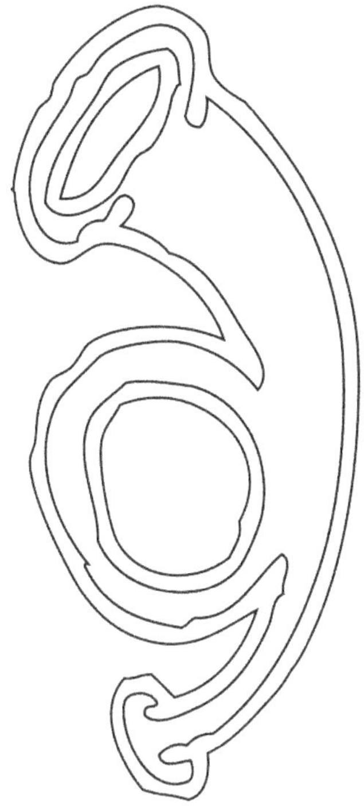

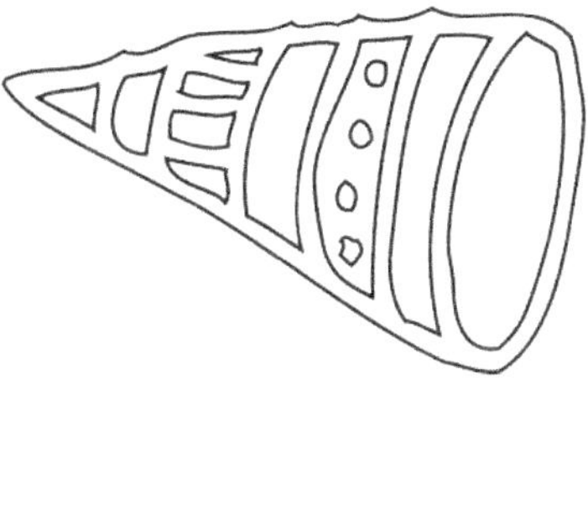

www.ingramcontent.com/pod-product-compliance
Lightning Source LLC
Chambersburg PA
CBHW081752280526
45789CB00008B/2831
* 9 7 8 1 5 3 9 9 4 3 8 0 8 *